First Confession

First Confession

Poems by

Sandra Kacher

© 2023 Sandra Kacher. All rights reserved.
This material may not be reproduced in any form, published,
reprinted, recorded, performed, broadcast,
rewritten, or redistributed without
the explicit permission of Sandra Kacher.
All such actions are strictly prohibited by law.

Cover design by Shay Culligan
Cover image by Sharon Waldron via Unsplash

ISBN: 978-1-63980-256-2

Kelsay Books
502 South 1040 East, A-119
American Fork, Utah 84003
Kelsaybooks.com

Acknowledgments

This book has been a mostly pleasurable journey of three years. I would like to thank June Blumenson, my friend, teacher, and poetry mentor, and Terry Lucas, my coach for the past year. In addition, I have much gratitude for Beth, Kathy, Cynthia, Liz, and Diane, members of my poetry writing groups, and for Susan, editor extraordinaire. It is a blessing to join the long line of people writing poetry. You have lifted me up in sorrow and enlivened my joy.

Adanna and Corvus Review: "Never Not Broken"

Better Than Starbucks: "Phlogiston"

Channel Magazine: "Trust"

The Galway Review: "Last Rites" (under the title "Dissolving"), "Disappointed"

Home: "Breakfast in the Neighborhood" (under the title "Breakfast at Brueggers")

Iris Literary Journal: "Tree Therapy"

Martin Lake Journal: "The Sweetness of Roadside Raspberries," "Winter Walk"

Star 82 Review: "Oaxaca Morning on the Way to Spanish Class"

We Were So Small: "First Confession"

Contents

I. Separations

First Confession	15
The Ache in Quarks	16
Never Not Broken	17
Communion	18
Last Rites	19
Rue	20
Pets and Other Losses	21
Give Us This Day	22
From a Grieving Womb	23
Marcescence	24
She Pours Coffee	25
Waiting for the Apocalypse	26
Disappointed	27
Oizys	28
We Don't Like Each Other Anymore	29
Was That Tree Here This Morning?	30
Losses	31
After Hans Christian Anderson's *The Red Shoes*	32
Tree Therapy	33
Earthbound	34

II. Consolations

Trust	37
Choose This	38
Who would have thought it could be so easy?	39
Give Us a Hand, Won't You?	40
Pocket Money	41
Phlogiston	42
Breakfast in the Neighborhood	43
The Sweetness of Roadside Raspberries	44

Mindfulness fails when you lose the knack of close attention	45
Oaxaca Morning on My Way to Spanish Class	46
The Poet Walks Her Dog	47
Early Spring Road Trip	48
Chop Wood, Carry Water	49
Sewing	50
Thomas at Four	51
Winter Walk	52
Arizona Highways	53
Wisdom	54
At Ninety	55
We Fall	56

I. Separations

You see this glass? For me the glass is already broken.
—Ajahn Chah

First Confession

What could she,
at seven,
have known of sin
when she entered
that curtained box,
knelt in dips
shaped by previous penitents,
heard the ominous slide
of the priest's grate,
felt the first rodent's gnaw
of guilt?

Is it blasphemy to lay
the idea of sin
onto the mind
of a child?
Or is it grace to
give her a name
for the dark self
she already knows?

The Ache in Quarks

Not a bang but an ache
launched the universe.
Before there was anything,
there was something
missing:
desire to *be with*—
the passion that drives
magnets to touch,
swells breasts to dripping,
hollows flutes
to caress the homesick ear.

Eyes the color of pining
tint the world,
ears tuned to melancholy
resonate to the sounds
of geese flying south.

The universe plays its deepest songs
in minor keys.

Never Not Broken

This lily at high summer noon—
tiger orange, fire orange,
perfect confluence
of year and day and light—
blazes in the heart of August.
At day's peak I foresee
the coming sunset.

Urged to dance in the light
not mourn in the shadows,
I try to flame silently
like an August lily.

But *Akhilandeshvara,*
the Goddess Never Not Broken,
is my saint. She tells me not to fight
the falling to pieces of everything
now or eventually.

At weddings they shun her,
she's barred from baptisms
and turned away from funerals
where the afterlife is praised,
the grief-stricken told
everything happens
for a reason.
She is wiser.

Don't get me wrong,
I love blazing,
but I know ashes, too.

Communion

As I kneel among gilded Marys and kindly Josephs,
a flat white circle sucks moisture from my mouth.
My tongue probes for Jesus in the scraps
of wafer stuck to my palate.

In this dissolving world, I look elsewhere for moisture—
snowflakes melting on lips
dew on clover,
fog scrolling around cattails,
rivulets trickling among boulders,
tears on my dying father's cheeks.

Last Rites

There goes the brittle need
to sparkle, its sequined cloak
a final glint in the sunset.

Edges blur, mordant wit
takes its last bite,
sensitivity clots and scabs—
a relief to shake off scarred feelings,
pride that's punctured daily.

Grief and solace battle as layered rags,
the costumes worn for this life's production,
drop away.

Un-feathered now,
shivering in my gooseflesh,
I come to the fear of the matter.

Easy to release the unloved,
but what about bougainvillea
vining up walls of cracked concrete,
magenta sparks gleaming
in early morning mist?
Baristas who remember my name
when I'm at my most invisible?
How my son-in-law comes up
with a namesake cocktail?
How I break out in curiosity
just when I think I'm forever jaded?

How do I say farewell
to the revelations of this rocky world
and the surprising sweetness of
myself?

Rue

You wrapped me
in a knee-squeezing hug
when you were three,
said you loved me fifty-seven times.
After the tenth, I turned back
to my overdue library book.

At four, you scaled my bed at midnight.
I wanted to pull you close,
but afraid to unman you
with too much tenderness,
I sent you to your room,
your footie pajamas
pale in the darkness.

At six, you helped me weed,
waved the slender stems
of creeping bellflower you'd uprooted.
We didn't know each piece of taproot
left behind would flower anew,
invasive as regret.

Pets and Other Losses

The sun blasts the windshield
and you cry, *"Turn it off!"*
At five, you believe I'm omnipotent.

You know I can't bring Dakota
back to life but insist I make
the heart pain end.

Do you remember
how you pointed to the spot
at the center of your chest?
How we both cried?

Tears for you have watered my life,
your sorrows' seeds sprout in me,
scatter dark-bright petals,
the bare stem bends.

Give Us This Day

If, for just one time,
I could sweep
the crumbs beneath the table
to a settled drift.
I might enjoy the challenge
of corners if the dust pile
would hold steady
when I lift the broom.
I did this yesterday,
I'll do it tomorrow, too.

I'd rather rest in not doing,
live in a house where morsels don't move.
I call on Aeolus, god of wind,
to hold his breath awhile
so I can catch my own.

I'd like a meal without mess,
self-cleaning woks and skillets,
dust-repelling coffee tables
and spices that alphabetize themselves.

I want neighbors
who rush to shovel my driveway
flowers delivered weekly
from an unknown admirer,
birthday presents every day.

I want to be a goddess
who observes the dear human creatures
stumble through their foolish, fallible lives
while I recline with grapes
and chocolate.

From a Grieving Womb

No more use for toddler
t-shirts and corduroys,
her older brother a ghost
mewing in every room.

With toes strung like pearls,
and tiny feet that drowned
in blue booties, her cries,
at first fierce and hopeful,
sank to sighs, then silence.

Mirrored only by emptiness
in her mother's eyes,
she grew insubstantial,
near twin to her missing brother.

A lion cub might claw through
jungle so thickly vined,
might grow to roar,
but she, a kitten,
had only light cat feet
and a gift for disappearing.

Marcescence

In these bleak November days,
leaves are torn from branches,
flung to the ground.

Marcescence, a leafy trick
to wither but not fall off,
allows whiskey-colored scraps
to dance shadows on January's white.
Some leaves abide long after October
flings their cousins down.

Will I linger past
my friends' departures?
Will I cling, shrunken and brittle,
desperate not to fall?

That withered leaf,
burnished to copper glint
in this late season light,
makes me burn to stay.

She Pours Coffee

into a stained white cup, checks
her Ameritrade account,
opens *Words With Friends,*
wracks her brain for something
that ends in q or z. The kitchen
is empty this morning, as every morning.
Her skin snags on the dry wood of her small table
as she brushes crumbs from the old pine.

Lips parched, fissured heels rasp,
she scratches a late season bite,
the thin skin of her ankle bleeds.

Cactus world she calls it and never knows
when a cholla will take aim and fire.

She dreams of a green life sprouting,
leafing, vining up the walls.
In a world of radiance
her skin inhales sunlight,
exhales laughter.

She taps in pizazz,
sighs, opens her 401K.

Waiting for the Apocalypse

On a day of ash and wormwood,
when seeds of barbed wire sprout
in the flowerbed, I bury my birth certificate,
burn wedding photos, listen to the death rattle
of leaves scuttling across the cracked driveway.

What to do with despair? Grate it
with cheese and melt it for fondue,
kiss spring's first violets, their dewy faces
rising above the mud of March.

Some bus riders will stand
to offer seats to old men
who lean on canes and mothers
with toddlers barnacled to their legs.
Is simple kindness enough?
Enough that bluebells return
each spring, and life carries on?

I watch November denuded leaf by leaf.
Someday the earth will green in April,
the breeze witnessed only by tiny hairs
on the backs of cockroaches

Disappointed

I break my dishes because they haven't saved me.

I looked to porcelain for clarity, stoneware for ballast,
neatly sorted cutlery from salad fork to steak knife,
made a nest for serving spoons.

There is no salvation in the kitchen,
no matter the number of seasonings,
the distance they traveled on the spice road.

I can distinguish aleppo from habanero,
cinnamon from cassia, but my tongue will tell you
you can't cook your way to heaven.

Oizys

Greek Goddess of Misery

Seventy now,
hating these jellied upper arms
jiggling on the open window frame
of a rusted Chevrolet.

As I bump along
a winding flinty road,
memories surface
from a dark heart-cave—

not a swimmer,
clumsy, self-banished,
shivering on the wet shoreline

self-culled from a cluster
of dancers' twirling skirts,
straightlaced among the ruffles

covetous, wistful
longing for my lost rhythm
exiled from my home planet

—my arms are beautiful.
I have missed my life.

We Don't Like Each Other Anymore

Once, bundled in a cloak
we wove from our delight,
warmed as winter stalked the hearth,
we lived fire-lit and golden.

Now, your downturned mouth demeans,
farewells yawn their boredom,
icicle words frost my lungs.

Smiles take more effort than sneers.
We no longer sand the edges off our words,
take three deep breaths or count to ten.
You plant harshness in everyone's garden,
while waves from my bad moods
crash into walls we built to shelter joy.

I watch the sun fade, dark arrives early.

Was That Tree Here This Morning?

Are you worried as I search in vain
for the word I knew yesterday
and will remember at midnight,
but can't locate as we sip our wine?

Should I clasp or swat the hands
that reach to help me down the steps?
Yesterday I tumbled from my bike—
falling was easier than getting up.

Friends say handsome men
no longer see them,
waiters forget to take their orders,
my sister was knocked to the curb
in a stampede of stiletto heels.

Memories flake like paint chips
from a rusting pole.
Salmon returning to their birthplace
swim with ease till they reach waterfalls
where they leap and fall back,
leap and fall back,
like neurons trying
to jump synapses,
find their way back
to memory's headwaters.

Losses

Some days there is only confusion
and a search for keys
somehow snatched in the night.

I know they're in the purse I bought
from a table near a bounty of rich cheeses
in a stall at a Paris market.
Nose pricks and mouth waters in memory.

Anyway, where is that purse?
And where did I lay my brush?
My hair would scare a crow
not to mention the birds with shining feathers.

Oh, it's all a mess. There must be answers
somewhere, though not in the rising panic
that tells me nothing lies head but dissolution.

It's not death but this slow dissolve
that terrifies me.

After Hans Christian Anderson's *The Red Shoes*

Desperate for what
was never given,
neither would stop
dancing,
not drop an arm,
nor step away.

Each thought the other
knew the steps
but wouldn't
take the lead,
held a prize
just out of reach,
let it sparkle
like sunlight on ice,
let it melt.

Tree Therapy

Outside my window, leaves are singing
the long green patience of trees,
rhyming their love of ground and sky.

I ask them—will they hear my stories,
dulled with telling, like the beads on my grandfather's rosary?

Every night he prayed the loops of Hail Marys
and Our Fathers, never doubting his words
would fly to heaven's gate.

I stir my morning coffee; steam rises only to my lips.
It's pepper that bites through the eggs.

In the mirror, narrowed eyes and downturned mouth
look back from a glass no amount of rubbing can clear.

Maple leaves speak of winters so cold
root hairs lick frost for months, summers so dry
roots snake down a hundred feet to tongue for drops of wet.

I ask the secret of their faith.
"We can neither turn away nor run."

Earthbound

Why don't aliens ever choose me
for an abduction? I'm despondent,
left behind in this ordinary world.

I'd like a few chips implanted,
one for teleportation, one for telepathy,
a third for merging with the Everything.
Where is my near-death experience,
so transformative, so elusive?

It isn't earth that limits me
as much as this suitcase of skin
that claims to be all I am.

Hard sides and zippers
encase me. Outside,
mandalas spin the universe
into harmony.

If not space travelers,
who will help me escape
this old valise?

II. Consolations

*And all shall be well, and all shall be well,
and all manner of things shall be well.*
—Julian of Norwich

Trust

Let it pour over you like rain
after seasons of drought, let perfume
from the thirst-quenched soil

fill your lungs. Let it hold you,
like mountain pines beside
treacherous roads, stopping your fall.

Let everything stop your fall—
the newborn's eyes barely open,
sunlight bouncing leaf to leaf,

gold butter wrapper scraped clean,
jam clotted on the knife that sweetens
your griddled toast, napkins that offer themselves

to your buttery hand,
receipt crumpled beside the plate,
light radiating from the long red hair

of a woman staring out a window.
All this on a table at ten in the morning,
stopping your fall.

Choose This

Why not fall in love
with this tattered,
fallen world?
True, it's not
of your design—
you might
have provided
more guardrails,
not seeded
bindweed among
the roses, or filled skies
with locusts
and further plagues.

But the mountains
are friendly
in a stern way
and the flat places
grow on you
if you let them.
Deserts offer
arid love and the
faces of elders
will shine if
you sit still
beside them.

You are wind that gusts
then drops away.
Why not shake
the trees
while you're here,
stir up some
gorgeous trouble?

Who would have thought it could be so easy?

Yes, who would have thought,
an ant could lead a platoon
to where the sugar hides

a tomato, tight and green
could plump up, fill with juice
tangy and sweet at once

dry wood could tender itself
to flame, surrender in a blaze
of orange and bright

this baby here could open
her space-dark eyes and smile
at the waiting world?

Give Us a Hand, Won't You?

a prayer to Kwan Yin—bodhisattva of compassion

You have a thousand of them,
each with an eye to gaze steadfast
on human suffering.

Your arms hold ten thousand
suffering souls, yet reach
for more. The Buddha
gave you eleven heads to fathom
such hardship. You turn a face
to the unmarked graves of children
buried on the grounds of Indian schools.
Tears stream down every cheek when
the thin white bones are raised.

How do you bear it, second after
never-ending second? Are your
eyes blistered? And your arms,
must you carry the children always—
a tribeswoman endlessly moving buckets
up and down the mountains,
knowing how throats parch and lips crack
without mercy's moisture?
Are you ever the nurse in a combat hospital,
sleeping only to dream of blood and gashes,
waking only to wrap another round of bandages?

Is there a sweet nectar that nurtures you
as you carry us? Will you take me
to that garden?

Pocket Money

An oak tree clothed in rough bark
evokes my mother's flea-bitten raccoon coat.
Its pockets jingled with quarters
captured in crumpled Kleenex.

She handed me the heavy coat
as a brace against north country campus winds.
Its weight comforting, its heft
slowed my tentative steps on glittery walkways,
safeguarded treks through crackles
of refrozen slush. I spent her coins
on coffee cups to warm my hands.

Raccoons, crafty scavengers,
steal scraps to feed their pups.
My mother scavenged wisdom
from a scrappy childhood in
the Great Depression:

Don't sniffle or God will give you
something to cry about,
black and navy blue,
will never go out of style,
clip seams when you're sewing curves,
never omit the basting.

She foraged a life from a hungry start,
filled boxes with fabric, sewed
clothes to dress a ragged heart.
With fashion advice surpassing wisdom,
she sent me off to learn what she hadn't.
Long after her departure, her gift warms me.

Phlogiston

I torched a sturdy branch last night,
dreamed beside its capering fire
till only embers remained.
Today I coax flame from
dry leaves and dull red cinders.

Phlogiston—essence of all
that sparks and blazes—
dabs of light in birch leaf coins
carpeting an October forest floor,
specks hidden in flint and jasper,
conjured by shaved steel and friction,
fire in silken fabric flaring
as sari'd women walk
in fields of sunflowers.

The leaves catch. A wood thrush
sings in morning's moist air,
a laughing man tips his hat,
children hold orange crossing flags
to guide the smalls to school.

My heart ignites.
Phlogiston.

Breakfast in the Neighborhood

I could live in this coffee shop.

The toddler with pulled up shirt
rubs his round belly,
performs a fat-bottomed downward dog,
takes a gentle tumble, laughs,
runs to the end of his mother's rope.

I want to befriend everyone here,
the jostling soccer team,
the texting girls, the boy
leaning against his dad,
learning to talk football,
the sleepy-eyed couple
shining on their newborn.

I love families that hug,
even the teenage girl and her father,
their magnets currently set on repel—
a different kind of hug.

In cafés in Budapest and Paris
glossy people down shots of thick espresso,
opine in glittering phrases.
I would feel smug if I were one of them.

But I don't live in a sparkling city,
I live where little boys express themselves
in toddler yoga, teenagers roll up jerseys
to reveal their abs, fathers with round bellies
pull their shirts firmly down, meet my eyes
and smile.

The Sweetness of Roadside Raspberries

You begin the run that
will finally turn your legs
to steel, give you power
for the marathon you've dreamed
of since you picked up
that *Runners' World* magazine
in your doctor's waiting room.

Your heart rate flashes on your wrist
and you see yourself leading to the finish line.
Pumping your legs, straining the bellows
of your lungs, focused on your running stats,
you push, unseeing, past rocks and smears
of streaming green. You don't see
that last night's rain washed the grasses
or notice the air is free
of yesterday's dust.

You go until the machine runs down,
buckle at the side of the road.
Breezes cool sweat that stings your eyes,
spiky weeds prod your arm,
raspberries still dewy with recent rain
moisten your dry mouth and
call you back to your body.

Mindfulness fails when you lose the knack of close attention

Magnesium   will relink my broken   synapses but only
            If   I   don't   forget to take it.

My phone is   gone again   with   no one home to
              dial my number.   I beagle around
            dining room   and bathroom,
                  peer into oven   and freezer.
Purse and car   are no-goes.

            I wonder,   is there   a universe
                  where nothing   is lost,
            only misplaced,
where the boy I loved   in seventh grade
                  lingers near my locker?
            And the crone   I'm becoming
                  laughs   with   shining eyes?

Oaxaca Morning on My Way to Spanish Class

I stumble on time-polished bricks
and broken pavement.
Buildings trumpet notes
of carmine and mustard,
marigold and sangria,
brilliant as the vegetable dyes
of Oaxacan rugs
too perfect for any floor.

Soft air soothes after a night strafed
by music from a girl's lavish *Quinceneara*—
all joy to her. The air tickles me awake,
I remember Fifteen—doors opening,
freedom teasing, rampant confusion,
my heart's bashful birdsong.

I want to tell her:
someday you will land here,
most of your choices made,
picking your fiestas carefully,
ambling toward the new language
you are loving to learn.

The Poet Walks Her Dog

Woodrow and I, new to the street,
launch ourselves down the porch steps,
eager to sniff out the neighborhood.

His first stop a palm tree, its trunk
scraped at the base, a gossip column
of local love and conflict. For me, a cluster
of poppies, orange petals are pages
of a book open in the wind.

We race past the oily skunk
of fresh-pressed asphalt.
At a metal street grate, he flops
and rolls. It looks so delicious,
I'm tempted, but I don't have
his yogi flexibility or self-forgetfulness.

I name and judge, he ambles along,
perfectly matches my stride,
breathes it all in,
lets it all pass.

Early Spring Road Trip

We enter Nebraska where spring green
climbs prairie grasses silvered over winter,
play tag with a dusty rig
lumbering along I-80,
wave as we pass him by.
The driver nods when he catches up.

Not much to do on this route.
When we stop to stretch, the wind
carries the horsey smell of the West
and I wonder should I have chosen
the life of a cowgirl swooping down
from the Sierras, always riding,
always moving the dogies along?

We played license plate tag
when I was small, the first
to spot Alaska got ice cream.
Now we spit out sunflower shells,
yawn, stare at stumps dotting the landscape
like age spots on a trucker's arm.

In the open place
between journey's start and finish,
possibilities billow.
In my next life, shall I be

cowgirl?

mustang?

mountain?

Chop Wood, Carry Water

a long day of log splitting and weed pulling,
a parade of powder post beetles
bolting from burrows
chewed through the hard wood

swiping sunburned faces
with rough bandannas
channels of dirt on reddened cheeks

clearing a plot for
raspberries and asparagus
plants that will stay
for twenty years

at night, shared silence
and the snap of burning juniper
punctuated by whimpers
from the dreaming dog

Sewing

I tell her the governor of New York resigned.
Pecking at her laptop, she ignores me.
I begin my stretches. She mentions
that the governor of New York just resigned.

I speak to the ceiling, she mumbles.
The wind knocks at the door,
carries her words to the lakeshore
where breakers swallow them.

We know each other so well—
how can there be any new stories?
It's been thirty years
since we recognized each other,

both unevenly mothered.
Today she speaks of new-found compassion
for the weary woman who did her best
for seven kids and an angry husband.

Too old to wear resentments rags,
we thread our darning needles.
Outside, waves shape and reshape.

Thomas at Four

Called by storms,
he maps Tornado Alley,
roars back at thunder,
reads by lightning bolt.

At four, he's planned his future:
chase storms then paint them.
His canvas will blaze
with the orange that spins
at the heart of every twister,
the fierce curiosity of orange
that flows through his veins
like magma.

Winter Walk

Throw out the dregs
of distraction,
involve yourself with grasses,
flowers in retreat,
birds gone silent,
stillness and space.

Look how hints
of sunrise blush and
moonrise blue
tint the snow.
Read sentences
written by boots
on unbroken white.
Dance to the half-time shuffle
of twigs tapping ice.
Cup icy water
whirling in the open creek.

In this unsullied winter,
breathe purity and rise.

Arizona Highways

We leave three hours late
for the long journey home,
snowbirds with ruffled feathers.

You are silent,
the road spools ahead.
I seethe beside you,
loser again in the battle over time.

In this landscape,
skeletal thistles cut the air,
everything pricks,
cacti prepare to fight.

Hearts of juniper wood
twist in mountain-scouring winds,
bleached grasses shrink
from trucks racketing by.
Rocks cluster like grave markings,
white crosses cry out in warning.

Parched and armed,
I sulk until you point
to the blue and yellow wildflowers
ribboning the highway,
tiny flowers that bloom
in rocky ground.

Wisdom

At twenty
you believe your supple body
will never stiffen,
deny that tears and laughter
will track your flawless face.

You know that everything wants to touch.
Bees dive thorax-deep into lavender blooms,
the breeze through summer's open window
caresses your nipples.
You explore the unlined face
of the lover who will warm the pillow
beside you until stalactites and stalagmites
consummate eons of desire, kiss at last
after a ten-thousand-year flirtation.

The first bang was a scattershot,
but every solitary neutrino—
whizzing outward on its lonely journey,
remembers the before time
when everything nested together.

At Ninety

So, here's the deal,
you're going to die.
But before that
most of the people you love
will get sick or leave.
You'll be alone in a cramped room,
the nurse will forget your meds
and a crazy lady in a blue denim dress
will pace up and down your hallway.
Every time you wave
she will ask your name.
The meat will be mush
and the peas tough,
you will play balloon volleyball
with a lot of old people.
At Christmastime they will
dress you in a red velvet cape
and make you sing, "Joy to the World."

Your death won't come soon enough,
the grapefruit juice will be delicious.

We Fall

a thousand times—

off a jagged curb,
over a buckling root,
from a roof we're patching with tarry shingles.
We tumble unharmed through thin air,
twist an ankle when we land,
get up and stumble on.

Heedless, taking a photo, I back off a cliff,
bounce boulder to boulder,
break and bloody my head,
land foot-first in a river roiled by water
that has thundered a thousand icy miles
to this place where I lie alone.

They come then, the green-clad foresters
with their red stretchers, pass me up, *up, up*
to hands waiting to slide me
onto a cot, narrow and white
amid wheezing pumps
and flashing screens. Small
I am then and shivering,
shards of fear splinter my thoughts.
An attendant lays a blanket warmed
for such disaster.

Hatchling in a nest of lights and wires,
but snug, strangely easy among hands
that check my vitals, a voice that whispers
You'll be all right—a promise
I've waited years to hear.

What we need in the emergency that is our life—
comrades to warm the cold and shattered places.

About the Author

Sandra Kacher loves poems that makes her smile but prefers those that bring her to tears. She is moved by "the crack in everything" especially when the crack plunges deep into mystery. She has lived most of her life in Minnesota—at twenty she discovered a part of Minneapolis she hadn't known existed and she's been looking for and finding hidden gems ever since. She loves seeing things for the first time but as she's lived in the same state for seventy years, she's learned that freshness doesn't require new geography, only open eyes and a desire to be surprised.

Fascinated by other people's stories, she spent her career as a psychotherapist listening to and being moved by those stories. She began writing poetry seriously once she retired and could no longer claim not to have time to write. Poetry is how she tells her own stories, and she invites you to please come in for a listen.

www.ingramcontent.com/pod-product-compliance
Lightning Source LLC
Chambersburg PA
CBHW030915170426
43193CB00009BA/865